HOUSES FLY AWAY

HOUSES FLY AWAY
POEMS BY LEIGH ANNE COUCH

ZONE 3 PRESS
Clarksville, Tennessee

ZONE 3 PRESS

Clarksville, Tennessee

Copyright © 2007 by Zone 3 Press

First Printing

LCCN: 2007926062
ISBN: 978-0-9786127-2-6

Cover and book design by ***David Bieloh***

Cover Art: "House Wren" ©2001 by
photographer ***Victor Schrager***

A Tennessee Board of Regents Institution

Austin Peay State University is an equal opportunity
employer committed to the education of a nonracially
identifiable student body. AP026/07-07/Thomson-
Shore/Dexter, MI

for Kevin, my dearest reader

ACKNOWLEDGMENTS

I gratefully acknowledge the editors of the following publications, in which the listed poems originally appeared, occasionally under different titles: *Alaska Quarterly Review*: "Missionary Ridge"; *Bark*: "the opposite of helium"; *Beloit Poetry Journal*: "Obsolescence"; *Blackbird*: "Luna Moth"; *Carolina Quarterly*: "What the Dead Say" ["Human History"], "Reach" ["Spring Monologue"], "To Be Fire," "Fish"; *Cimarron Review*: "When Memory's Like That House in *The Violent Bear It Away*," "Nest"; *Cincinnati Review*: "Attraction," "Daughter Dreaming Tornado"; *Distillery*: "Goldfinches"; *The Eleventh Muse*: "The Eleventh Hour," "Ciphers"; *Greensboro Review*: "Maid," "The Bed Is a Still Life of Flying"; *Louisville Review*: "Trains"; *Nimrod International Journal*: "Vanishing Point"; *Painted Bride Quarterly*: "the finale of be"; *Seattle Review*: "Fossil Love"; *Sewanee Theological Review*: "Elegy for Snow"; *Shenandoah*: "Palm Reader Sees Long Love"; *Slope*: "Camel Stamp," "Astronaut" ["Quake—Heart"]; *Southern Poetry Review*: "Minor Season"; *storySouth*: "Perpetual Care at Plainview"; *Verse Daily*: "Obsolescence" (reprinted); *Western Humanities Review*: "Beast"; *Whiskey Island Magazine*: "Lazarus," "neither created" ["matter & tea"].

CONTENTS

v   Introduction / Writing To Be a Field

1   Beast

3   Allegory 1968
4   Daughter Dreaming Tornado
5   Trains
7   When Memory's Like That House...
9   Estrangement
10 Goldfinches
12 Absence
14 the finale of be
15 coda

16 encore
17 Tideland
19 Elegy for Snow
20 What the Dead Say
22 The Eleventh Hour
23 Perpetual Care at Plainview
24 Luna Moth
25 Lazarus
26 Obsolescence
27 Fish
29 Edisto
30 The Opposite of Helium
32 Neither Created

33 Short History of White Flight
35 Maid
37 Blight

39 Vanishing Point
40 Astronaut
41 Slide
42 Missionary Ridge
44 Nest
45 Reach

46 The Bed Is a Still Life of Flying
48 Ciphers
49 Sighting
51 Fossil Love
52 Minor Season
53 To Be Fire
54 Interleaving
55 Attraction
56 Palm Reader Sees Long Love
57 Camel Stamp

58 Notes
60 About the Author

WRITING TO BE A FIELD

Giacomo Leopardi, the great nineteenth-century Italian poet, once wrote that the best poems "even when they give a perfect likeness of the nullity of things, even when they clearly demonstrate and make us feel…the most terrible despair,…they always serve as a consolation, rekindling enthusiasm, and though speaking of and portraying nothing but death, restore to it, at least for a while, the life that it had lost." What the Romantic Leopardi was getting at is art's incredible power to transform and to metamorphose, to create a world that, if it does not replace ours, at least offers us a parallel existence. The poet becomes a kind of Pygmalion who returns home to kiss poetry's representation of an alternate world, and finds it real.

For the poetry of Leigh Anne Couch this return and transformation radiates outward in concentric circles: the opening poems try to find ways to transcend the physicality of a mortal world, followed by poems that attempt to regain the lost past through memory, and finally poems that negotiate ways to settle for a transient love as a form of possessing the world. For example, in one poem, "Nest," a woman in a hospital room confronts an unknown sickness which is partly a metaphysical nihilism. In the end, she will be discharged, but the freedom from her condition is only temporary:

> Waiting for the papers
> that say she can go, knowing she'll be back
> in a month, she jerks up the blinds,

could make someone bleed, and there,
dozens of hornets, drugged in August heat,
circle and circle their papery catacombs,
the color of someone dying for years.

The intensity of the scene is produced by Couch's subtle
mastery of language: the way the bleeding is projected onto
the blinds, and the very tactile description of the nest. The
window provides no escape—the blinds are like cell bars—
and the drugged hornets reflect her own condition: her very
life is a catacomb. And yet this desperation is immediately
countered in the next poem ("Reach"): "Take my hand from
my mouth and I might start singing."
　　This counterpointing of images and ideas provides Couch's
verse with enormous tension. The aim is, from the ve ry first
poem, to find a way to synthesize physical and metaphysical
things and what we make of them, through language:

We poke around the grass, the sun warms
our skins, we make more of ourselves, we eat,
don't get eaten, sleep—it's enough for a life.
To taste the shape of that—enough—
to mouth its escape and take one more breath
as it struggles, wings against the teeth.

From thing to taste to shape to utterance: each stage is
perhaps enough, but never finally enough. There is always
the struggle to go beyond. It is a gesture that must keep
being uttered, as later in "The Bed Is a Still Life of Flying,"
where a woman is dreaming that her bed becomes by turns a
"still life" of "pitching seas," of "driving off bridges," and of
several other scenes. It is as if by envisioning her life as a

composed picture of memories and anticipations she can imagine "a still life of dying, /...a still life of flying" as she waits "for her body to return." As she says in "Trains," "part of what you are is what you aren't."

The paradoxical nature of her language gives Couch a vision that realizes how "One by unique unknowable one we scatter / and return to a drift of souls" and yet at the same time hopes that "the sea...remembers why we came" ("Elegy for Snow"). But memory always falls short, and any real and final revival of the past is always disappointing. In "Lazarus," for example, the revived person "ate regularly, / said little, and watched the windows," while he toys with a cocoon and kills the possibility of life within it. And yet the language always strives for the impossible—in a poem titled "Fish," Couch uses a metaphor of the world that "batters at the heart like a baby bird," mixing metaphoric contexts to jar us out of the sense that we exist on one plane. Such similes, like all her metaphors, send us off in disparate directions as if the very language, the very texture of the poems, is predicated on somehow attempting to escape the mortal condition we ultimately know we can't escape. Grief comes on "like an old film," the "refrigerator gnaws through the morning" consuming what it should preserve, and there are "crows hammering inside her chest." Images such as stones, gardens, clothing, beds, the body are constantly counterpointed against images of fields, windows, seas in order to suggest a sense of confinement and the need to transcend it. This is a vision of inescapable paradoxes where "What we thought we possessed, / possesses us" and where "the interior [becomes] exterior."

It is in the last part of the book that Couch finds a tentative synthesis of her paradoxes. For example, "Fossil

Love," as the poem is titled, suggests a kind of permanence, a "field of memory," and yet can be had only through extermination. But the ability to write about it provides at least a temporary triumph. Like the woman in "Minor Season" who "gathers patience / misshapen stones to keep hands busy," who begins to feel a "semi-transparent" light— "a mouth a face a moon"—we can "scribbl[e]," write, and recreate, capture the past. "I write field to be a field," the next poem asserts. The acts of writing themselves, all those subtly stirring metaphors, create not an idealized, romanticized world, but one that settles for the temporality of attachments, a Wordsworthian victory built of failures. These are poems that ask, finally:

> Am I your despair, and love an insoluble crystal.
> As field might exist to hold back the ocean[.]

"Holding back" is the realistic vision the book finally settles for. It is a kind of paradoxical stoicism, one that does not stop hoping for more. Walter Benjamin once wrote, "What seems paradoxical about everything that is justly called beautiful is the fact that it appears." And that, to be sure, is the ultimate beauty of this superb book.

Richard Jackson
University of Tennessee at Chattanooga

BEAST

I have good friends and a family
only slightly perforated. I eat three
maybe four square meals a day, still
the bird in my mouth, I long for—
not a scissor-tailed swift or jay
with perfect coiffure, but a little
leaf-round one, a warbler or sparrow,
a confection through the glass,
to run my tongue along its unmarrowed
bones, up under the chest of feathers.
I keep my teeth clean, floss nightly.
My wife and I are tender. I have a dog
who wants to please with tiny blind
animals dug from the neighbor's yard.
Still, the bird in my mouth—
the heart bumping the soft body,
tricycle lurching, a gravel road.
We're never alone with these
thousand Jonahs. They sing,
the squirrels and house cats too,
the wet vole at my feet, even the dog,
they sing to me: you are there, there,
there's nothing we think to do about it.
We poke around the grass, the sun warms
our skins, we make more of ourselves, we eat,
don't get eaten, sleep—it's enough for a life.
To taste the shape of that—enough—
to mouth its escape and take one more breath
as it struggles, wings against the teeth.
I take only what's given, what I can get,

and I get lonely in this body lost
in trees and air. To open my lips
slowly, pass my tongue through its cage,
I promise to let the pretty thing go.

ALLEGORY 1968

The Day of the Dead
The Day of All Souls

when people opened their doors, who are you,
and mothers checked apples for razors.

Without a name, I was meaning—
the lame one, feet bound by a wild-eyed mother.

I had a twin. We were taken to the jungle,
laid down in scratched-out troughs of moss and rot.

Sliding on bare floor like a piece of soap,
a baby slipped between the baseboards.

My name could have been Atlanta.
I was born in a waiting room.

The room was an orange maze of slatted cribs.
The squalling child or the sleeping child, I was

dropped into one of them
dropped into all of them.

DAUGHTER DREAMING TORNADO

Her ribs might pop like shoelaces but she could hold
her breath in water, warm like August and blood.
Her unstinging eyes float to the surface, blink
at the room's confusion, a dozen arms or the wings
of beautiful ravens, her parents undoing it all
because they'd hidden the brightest pieces from
themselves: forgotten their names, where the bedrooms were,
and how many children. Suddenly dear
the knickknacks in their places, suddenly heartbreaking
their places, a ring of dust, a skirt of wax.
Excuse me—too late to find the dreamer—Sorry.
Gentle Furies, Winged Voices, The Furiously
Blinking Eye, take your seats for the dream
within the dream: these parents made
it real with wanting, lives stacked dangerously
high with effects, choices they made or neglected
to make, but the child knows years don't pile up
or waste away, they pull, they strain—every
second born deforming the little ones
before. She wills them to remember her,
but they look back and see everything
just as it was. Into the greenish air,
nails explode, hot rain hisses on the tile.
Untouched and barely damp, she watches the house
fill with thunder and fire and learns her lesson:
Withstanding and letting go, the frame will fold.
She will wait—being made for this.

TRAINS

I don't know a thing about trains
but I felt the air change, roll under
the tidal wave of tonnage—metal sparks,
arms and foreheads. I looked up
Guttersnipe, it said *Street Arab.*
I went to *Patriot*, it came from *Father.*
I went to *Terror* which came
from *Fear*—it said, see *Tremble,* as in,
The building trembled from the blast.
I don't know a thing about trains
but their torn call, their melodeon gasping
like polished maple against my skin,
like stage cries of a drowning diva—
maybe no one hears them but me.
Ghosts from the 18th, 19th, 20th centuries,
has anyone told them they're a dying breed.
I don't know a thing about it. I do know
there was a belly of fire and the mouth of hell
a man in overalls opened and closed
on Sunday westerns I watched with my father—
the disappearing man on the backporch
of the red caboose waving *so long* to all of us.
I looked up *Caboose—A room on a ship*
which makes its own sense,
that part of what you are is what you aren't—
no matter how blue the ocean dreams you,
how empty the wind wants you to be—
part of me is dead and my father alive.
A train, like war, isn't dead or alive or dreaming.

It's fire, steel, tracks, almighty progress.
As for the words—without mouths and hands,
without love, hate, memory, words are fucked.
What if I put my love on that train.
What if people were laid down on the tracks
and we stood by, hands at our sides, mouths open
with the nothing we know about it.
War is from Old High German for *Confusion*.
Declare from Latin *To make clear and bright*,
like the day in September, blue
on your tongue, I mean it was perfect—
a girl skipping rope in Brooklyn
at the park by the river—Palestine, Oklahoma, New York,
                              D.C., Kandahar, the Gaza Strip.
The thing about trains that long,
she's never even heard one,
doesn't know they get louder, seem closer,
in winter when trees are bare.
She hops like a bird, looks at the skyline:
If the train should jump the tracks,
do you want your money back?

WHEN MEMORY'S LIKE THAT HOUSE IN *THE VIOLENT BEAR IT AWAY*
(and what the walls would say)

Pushed far to the back of a kitchen drawer
in the heart of a vacant house is a blue tin-box
two inches by two. If you got this far
you'd open the door, the drawer, the box,
you'd see a stone like a small ear
and a broken-out tooth hidden there.
The house you wouldn't see from the road.
Some nights the moon's been swiped with tar,
some days the house needs winding up.
Its memory smells like rancid flowers,
leaves beetle tracks in the dust.

For weeks someone squatted here dreaming of a chair.

How long has it been? *Look in your hand.*
Clutching a drop of liquid to its chest, the stone
is more alive than the tooth because it never was.
A leaf twirled in a river moving light,
and your insides swam that day like fish:
there you were after such a long time,
so you took the stone, one still thing.
The other, does it ring, the impact
of remembering? Does it dazzle in
the brainpan, a teacup smashed to bits?

I am a place where things come together then fly apart.

The house walks over, its doorway slips
around your shoulders, its threshold slides
under your shoes. You are the room
and its ghost feeling the walls, wanting
to latch the doors because this is love
remembering you—a robin's egg in the freeway.
The evidence in your hands: the tooth, the stone, the box.
You are the maker, the keeper, the finder,
this house of memory your embraceable prison.
Through the watery glass, a cough, a moon—
the slimmest light cradles its own dark—your hand
to your cheek, your tongue to the salty space.

Each day the story begins again and falls
to the middle, which passes out in the end. Try
to be careful, don't waste the heart, it wastes itself,
honeysick and hungry, you never disobeyed
desire, the ocean always comes back for more.
Dead, you won't have to try so hard.
Dead, your prospects are clear.
Leave it alone, let the sun slip down the black wall.
There are trains and soup pots boiling over,
high tides at night and behind the swells, an azure moon.

ESTRANGEMENT

In the plum-thick air a stranger takes halting steps downhill.
        The train's approach and cry.

I watch him through the needling late-time, beyond the circles
        inside—the chronic silences and women's arms
worn out with yearning for our brothers, husbands, fathers
        unwilling to be with us.

Their stubborn refusals ate the yard like privet root.
The fields they'd plowed exploded with onion and Bermuda grass.

        I haven't known a man who tried hard enough.
So far from me now, my father, I can't see if he's returning or hurrying
        away through chimney-shadows, but I can say

this stranger on the street has just been told he will die,
        and I can let my father be
his chrysalis trailing behind, lungs heaping and clean
        as new sails in the March wind.

This one would learn how to die and he'd teach me: *breathe*
steam rising off bruised plums. Nothing more. Cicadas burn in the trees.

GOLDFINCHES

The day was a goldfinch
beating wings
against a dirty cotton sky.
The sky swung low on the line.

My mother came to me,
an offering of her body. She
wasn't one to make such gestures.
My mother came to me, holding out ·

her left arm turned over,
soft underside, talcum-white.
She could have been a child. *Look*
she said, *Look*. But I was boxing

remembrances, worrying over what
I'd need, and nothing was here
in the scented damp around her.
The days were emptying,

self after self from her hands,
daughter, mother, wife, her fingerprints
slipped in someone else's milk after
years handling chemicals in the dairy lab.

Germs are everywhere, she'd say—
incubating in the ice cream, lurking
in lids and glasses. How could she sleep
through the furious racket

in my father's lungs, the merciless labor.
She came to me late that unquiet
summer when windowpanes screeched
and weeds withered at her glances.

I was the fruit that would not fall,
the sapling meant to stay faithful
to its roots, branch for branch.

For the settling of her fragile bones,
for the window-light stroking the bend
of her arm, for the warm blue pulse,

I would leave to find her in her father's
cornfield, the beautiful creases,
my mother's body filled with dirt.

Two girls, light, impossible,
roll through the furrows lengthwise,
close their eyes laughing,

pillow-feathers on a sheet
shaken out wave after solid wave
to the robust sky, like that forever.

ABSENCE

Stone
When I call to your smokehouse and fields,
your radio tubes and rusted tools,
what are you now but in pieces:
the place set at the end of the table,
the clothes laid out for you every day,
the dirt-and-mentholatum stained pillow, this stone
held against my chest, the weight
of your arm flung across me as we napped
through untroubled afternoons. Palm to palm—
one callous, a knot of arthritis, the other mine.

Garden
to find one soul out of so many
tongue-cut sparrow in garden-air
streaming noiselessly through
trees and rocks set like dishes
for tea in absence sliding
like mercury through fingers
of raked sand the character of the sea

Night
The flapping tent, a lady preacher
bent down to your granddaughter
in black: starlight starbright he'll be
the first you see tonight. Because
wishing hard is as good as prayer
I opened my eyes to the eastern sky broken
with light: thousands of stars, the souls of
strangers, had crowded you out.

Light
How far would I go
before the sky would give,
ripple to the touch,
dye my skin and hair blue?
With you gone, heaven is pure
emptiness, and a star nothing
but an open place,
brilliant chink out of night's army
of boulders, shouldering one another,
ominously close, barely keeping us intact.

the finale of be

to Wallace Stevens

when the heart is a trout pushing upstream
pre-life (life) post-life (life) pre-life (life)

and the sun a paralytic struck with a useless notion
its terrible eye fixed on me

whoosh go the memorable memories
the walls come a tumblin' down

the Mississippi-size blue of my self
gurgles through the featureless plain

a great irresistible soak
would nothing resist, something meant to be weightless

a child I thought all the babies
all the babies were tucked in the middle

in the middle of brides
now and instead curled

in the folds of knowing unknowing
nourished by DNA and what we can make

a soul slowly rouses
one day to wriggle free

overturning every wheelbarrow
slick with fungal water

coda

I don't know the body
if it has to die or the mind
be denied for the soul to show up

there's not much to go on,
not nature, the ocean, say,
pummeling rocks like a blind drunk

not religion's taxidermy shop
where being (here) then not
get gutted and stuffed

their eyelids smoothed out their bones
bent in repose
arranged for us tourists in judgment-day tableau

the bear cub shall ride the bobcat
into heaven and the beaver lie down with the fox
while the orange deer of meaning

track valentines
through blue snow
to the saltlick

encore

your sighs
my torso damp
and covered with touches
are sensational aren't they

the way we cave in shuddering
shake our heads no no
to empty rooms
half in love with our

velvet rope and chamber
wet lips, long limbs
our skin warmed again
to nutmeg and apricots

the body is the body
its longings pure to know
the finale of seem

where outside the treeline of stars
soft as dying in your sleep
the soul sneaks out before morning

TIDELAND

A body moves through still water.
Silk torn. Liquid wings.

One word, its trough and crest—
a wave lengthening to the shore.

She feels the land in its sway,
the one being lived by me.

The first compulsion of tides
began in still water, limitless

as black heaven, death,
an echo answering itself.

Springs come alive beneath the rind
ramifying through earth at our fingers'

touch on ten thousand fruits and more.
We bite and smear the juice, its scent

on our bodies, immortal in the calculus
of infinite variations on could have been.

Fly away blackbird. Nothing ends
once it's over. Split open

the clam to rude saucers:
grit pearl in one, salty eye in the other.

The eye-meat, what happens.
The pearl, what never ceases.

Fly away crow. Cast love out
and he'll be yours forever.

You'll harbor him like a felon
forgiving him again and again

till he's purified.
Death would be better,

my father winks
from his '79 Buick Skylark.

Come back to me blackbird.
Clamshells turn to wings.

Sky water. Ocean water. Spring water.
Orpheus sung to pieces.

What we don't live and what we do.
Connect syllable to deed, release

every word lined up like the young hoplites.
Let them stream from both sides of Thermopylae.

ELEGY FOR SNOW

Where the snow falls by thousands into the sea.
—Thomas Lovell Beddoes

A friend of a friend in my graduating class lost himself
near South Pittsburg, Tennessee. Alone
on the last day of the year, he swerved
on ice, to miss a deer, a dog, the shadow
of a dog, or to hit the tree that rammed
the steering column into his chest. His chest,
like a boy's at thirty, small-boned and pale,
a skeleton of wings, a fish. I remember
him shirtless, causing a stir as he swung
and veered on rollerblades down University,
his long silvering hair tangling behind:
always in motion and like the current
just past understanding. No chance now
to stop him, take him in, or whatever we try
on lost souls, no more lost than any of us:
a shred of wind, the heart's arrhythmia, flakes of shale
and silver falling up to fall down to hit bottom.
One by unique unknowable one we scatter
and return to a drift of souls waiting for dissolution—
and the sea, we hope, remembers why we came.

WHAT THE DEAD SAY

La Specola, Florence

In this city where streets are secret rooms,
at the bottom of six steps, a low-ceilinged gallery
waits for us—a wax display of flesh and bone
where the body is a wickless candle. The animals

are waiting; a tree in a field of wax and a sea
that could melt are waiting; but more than the others,
Paolo and Francesca draped over dusty crimson pallets
are waiting, enthralled under glass by our pitiful beauty.

A loose plait of real hair warms Francesca's left arm,
Paolo's eyes are half-drawn in a pleasurable doze.
Their abdomens cleanly split and organs pried out,
their pea-sized glands fixed in dark niches

like coins in a sofa. Here are the intestines, testicles,
uterus, glass eyes, fingernails, but where
is the soul? Immortality must be essentially a burden
to the living, our chain-mail cape, the dead

on our backs—metal clinks and fastenings
deaf to their own resurrections in our words
and laughter—they jangle through the years ahead
like change in a pretty girl's pocket.

Corsica

She rubbed bay on her hands and sage
on her body so wild horses would take her in.
When her shining mane turned
to wires of tarnished silver, and her skin
cracked like a fresco, she said with bitter wonder,
This is the privilege of my life,
to visit the birthplace of the man who broke me
and know he was my last only love.

Chapel Hill

Time reared up on its haunches and pounded away
to a dorm room where five kids died in a fire
that never touched their bodies in posed disarray:
one twisted and reaching behind the sofa, another

slumped against the wall like a drunk storyteller.
Would his Roman soul speak of the city of sarcophagi—
the sudden statues, where a woman in flight balances a cask
on her head, and a starving dog skulks to find his master?

These gnarled fingers and opened mouths of dailiness
tell us backward and forward,
What you have now forever you will have.

THE ELEVENTH HOUR

Blackflies and cornflowers, sour breath and delight,
circling ourselves circling the sun, the river's mania downhill,
the unretractable silences of a dying marriage, continental drift,
birdshit, bugshit smeared across the windshield, maps folded badly,
waking sore and twisted but grateful the bed has emptied
of those tidal contentments and gut instincts, noisy digestion,
fear like a vaccine, a hand over your mouth, a hand up your skirt,
Pol Pot and evangelical democracy, the day's news,
dirt on your thumbs, shame and faceless, wordless suffering,
the lesser evil, the greater good, feeble relatives, sodden guilt,
a baby fevered and squalling, self-made heroes crawling
to the top of the world, sound bites and touched-up photos,
pastel bodies propped against an affectless sea.
Dressing ourselves up for stories to be retold to ring true,
just before midnight, with the chance that we'd live again
given what we know, we would choose this razor's width,
this hair's breadth away—our innocence, the closest
we'll come to a god who does not disdain us.
In the eleventh hour we'd take it all again in one lump sum
while there on the floor of the ocean—where no light
bawls and form dissolves into slow tragic wavelengths,
where one of us with titanium lungs will be crushed
in the primitive action and reaction—a Timex,
like a bland-faced monk, crosses and uncrosses its hands,
having worked its way off a dead guy's wrist
as he struggled with the biggest catch of his life.

PERPETUAL CARE AT PLAINVIEW

Think of her as Chronos.
Think of her as Carrion.

She sleeps standing up, eats only seed,
gives fearsome little smiles with her teeth

remembering our electric skin, how we moved through
days cramming them in: starving in a field of berries.

Honoring us, the newly satisfied, the recently
out of time, she ties her dandelion hair in chiffon

and walks to Plainview where she touches stone
shoulders attentive at last. You're old longer than

you're young and dead longer than that. This is her calling.
She hears us calling. She'd crawl from the cemetery home

to care for her old children gone. She minds her steps
through our lengths and widths, goes quietly to the business

of tucking us in, trimming the yards with stubborn shears,
breaking up clods of dirt with her hands, and straightening

the waxed carnations on shaky legs, her weather-beaten
chorus still poised to sing, *you'll miss everything.*

LUNA MOTH

My father was rarely corrupted by pain

cared for exquisitely
through the hole in his arm

he settled into peace
shuffled its paces through the house

remembering him works like a mechanism
engaged : his white grip

on the metal bar, his voice smeared
on tape, the unrolling cylinder, the needle

pump, click and flash
of four rolls of film

he took from the bed
he finally would not rise from

these captives of sunlight
what couldn't be said at every slant

of day against the filthy buildings
peering in the hospital window

each photo signed at the bottom
by the bed's aluminum railing

and a cheap carnation of light
the sole point of clarity

LAZARUS

Till now in the airless dark, Lazarus
had no idea love means
thick blood in bruising blows
to the hands, feet, organs,

and mind—all coming to
like blind worms in a flood.
He tears at the winding sheet, rips it
from the mouth. Spiced air

cuts down to the lungs, choking
with the smell of his own decay.
He unwraps the arms, the torso,
the legs—glistening with aloe

from women's hands circling
his tightening body. God
returns him, just like that,
to his family's hysterical arms,

eels slapping loose skin.
Words slid down his throat.
Having felt nothing for four days,
what was there to say, even to Jesus?

After he died, he ate regularly,
said little, and watched the windows.
From the sill he picked off a cocoon,
popped it open with a long thumbnail.

He watched the wet opal covered in dust.
It finally stopped squirming.

OBSOLESCENCE

Precious is the crackslam of metal buttons in the dryer.
Families race room to room when telephone sings.
Bookshelves turn to wallpaper and we cherish the spines
standing at attention in their tidy jackets.
Through one-way preprogrammed interactions, we've fallen
in collusion with things and marvel at their loyalty,
their wrought-iron faith in us. In the archdiocese of spoons
there are no sinners, and saints are quaint but outdated technologies.
The wireless kingdom has come to install the earthly throne
of God; morning birdsong, the serpent's sigh, are hereby
preempted by the militant hmmm and murrrr, herds
of zip drives and other everlasting denizens of the new
paradise. Onward current flowing, Eden never sleeps.
We are the gardeners who might have been the garden.

FISH

You pull in the end of a summer day slowly,
and the long line pools in the middle of itself.
Late light streaming through each plume
of open wing, a thrush hesitates, tilts
and disappears. Six to eight o'clock is a length
of eternity and the inevitable waits. Don't
wait—move through the lowing, the train
in the distance coming or going, the indolent light
leaning on cars, fences, street signs—see it through.
See the light, like seeing a pretty girl home.
It passes through windows like water.
It won't outlast its welcome, and if that girl
comes to the window, its fingers reach
for her skirt politely. Easiest to feel
Eliot's stern comfort in these couple hours:
time and more time in-folded when all
manner of thing shall be well.
You want to believe the proof of heaven
is the slow smothering of years, our lifetime
of resisting, say time is not our ocean.
But what fish spends its short life building a boat?
Forty thousand stories through the dark,
the light comes still and what fish follows it
to the surface, swimming straight up until
choked and blinded by the sun? Say time
is not our ocean, this world not our home,
but it batters at the heart like a baby bird,
no eyes, a jerk and flutter on the pavement.
The houses are all gone under the sea.

The dancers are all gone under the hill.
You might not remember any of this.
You might get back every wasted second.
Just not yet, in this summered expanse
from six to eight o'clock when light, not time,
is our ocean. Day holds its breath forever
swimming lazily to the bottom
before night reels you in against another:
as one body you pace and turn
on a floor polished black-water deep—
a mirror mirroring the going under.

EDISTO

Palmetto leaves cut the sky to pieces
in blues sharp as the cicada's cry.

Slashes of heat on white planking.
Spanish moss like corpse-hair and a bare

mattress hanging from a live oak.
The sun backbends into dusk

and the god who loves unlovingly
unseams us, beginning

from end, water from air, amber
from ash on the horizon.

Families disappear. One by one
pelicans rise from the water

slowly beating the night-ready sky,
shadows trawl the beach.

Where will they rest? Light
closes down. The sea comes on.

THE OPPOSITE OF HELIUM

for Milton

A place in the yard, your property and province
of sunlit Saturdays when dirt and grass
held the warm shape of you down
into evening: a place beneath the birdfeeder,
the half-alive sweetgum, the fall sky, the cold
taking its time. I watched you turn over
like a piece of toast: you on your side
in the strong sun, the round Earth floating,
we were each other's child.

You pooled in such light, even your heart
grew drowsy. I took care, lost and found
you again and again. Hyperbole couldn't
squeeze in. Love was a helium balloon
in a room of opened windows.
Words would never follow.
You in the lead on barely beaten deer-trails
to the roots of a dead tree.
Some days we lived like squirrels.

Your gaze, the surface of a lake, gave
and received my fictions: cursed boy, student
of French, dashing silent-film star,
my most unpoetical Frankenstein,
Keats's beautiful return, and why not,
a life of Sensations rather than Thoughts!
Then no life at all when the setting sun
sets us to rights, to bone and ash on the shore

still too heavy for flight. Not being
mine, my 7 a.m., 5 p.m., midnight,
who are you? *Here baby, come on, let's go.*

They brought you to me on a silver cart.
Your body had grown a garden
of stars that wouldn't stop blooming.
I smelled garlic, warm butter, aftershave,
wild onion, dirt, smoke, formaldehyde, witch hazel,
my wristbones ached with blood,
your forehead fit perfectly in my palm.

This winter the birdfeeder brought a mess of cardinals.

Males drop from the sweetgum like kerchiefs.

The old black cat with the loose belly skin lurks there for hours.

NEITHER CREATED

He thinks of her mouth with the last swallow when the teabag slips
down the china cup, collapses to his tongue. She thinks of his voice,
crumbled leaves and falling in ochre liquid. Between them the air
thinks *skin is a vanishing that holds its breath.*

They turn, they're almost touching:
call and response, bamboo and sugarcane,
the finches rise up, one body eastward,
an empty sack twines in the wind,
the wick thrives in its crematory;
matter and tea, steamed gauze, leaf mold,
rarefied humus and peat, an unkempt garden
of magenta blooms steeped in rain and sunlight;
will and longing, the scent of a backyard
wind curls out from a pile of leaves
scattering hundreds of hands
waving themselves down—
each to the other, *I will not*
go away, you will not go away.

SHORT HISTORY OF WHITE FLIGHT

Gun barrels shining, huge in their arms,
deer-blood smudged their teacup faces,
my first students smiling from snapshots
taken where the land doesn't remember a thing,
but its people think they do—how parlors
swooned, tobacco was king, Brer Rabbit
held his sides in the briars, and black
women ate mud, slipping out
in gunnysack dresses, following
the moon's satin trail to the river,
pocketing spoons to scrape out clay
and swallow it down to their children.
How the speculators strolled
through town in reconstructed glory
when this pale dirt, this fat vein
of kaolin, was bottled and sold as Kaopectate!
Cruising the factories at night, the kids
made out under rows upon rows
of fluorescent lights throwing blue shadows
on ivory mounds like plugs of the moon,
a city full of crushed statues.
The years were pure cocaine,
cotton, a bleached page, desiccated
clouds, the flag of a deer in flight,
and a boy, his father shot dead in a bar,
who sat there in American Lit
coughing up expletives, spitting
laughter at *their eyes watching God.*
He came at night, threw rocks at my porch,

rattled the screens to see me jump.
Early spring. Honeysuckle dusk.
The sheets, just hung, pulled in the breeze.
I closed my eyes, a rifle clicked,
and I slipped slowly inside the horizon of ash
back to the South I'd call mine; my tires
were ravenous for the broken lines out of there.
None of us get justice by these fields,
mute and demanding. What we thought we possessed
possesses us, pulls us headlong
into illusion, like ribbons of water adrift
over the scalding highway snaking
through hills and swatches of pine,
past the Cullowhee's banks where men
might still be up to their necks in white
dirt to soothe a troubled system
born of the almanac, the family
Bible, the perpetual struggle to preserve
itself, the serpent nears its own
tail—*don't tread on me.*
In my rearview mirror, a hunter's moon,
nickel-small in the blue-black sea,
was blind, hot, and big as it will ever be.

MAID

Every knob and top serene with lemon oil, she snaps
up the top sheet; it falls satisfied on the bed,
unpuckered, primly tucked under.

Her order, not religious. The hereafter, inconsequential.
Life's the great mysterious. The least she can do
is show gratitude, offering her best,

which Mother called her sweetness. Confessing in low tones
to four rooms, four beds, four toilets
and sinks—her sins to statuettes turn;

she handles them over and over in her apron pocket,
knows them blind and featureless. Her lips
part and close with the recitation of flaws

until every fine bauble is dusted, down to the delicate
ballerina she saves for last, carefully wiping
the china hair, winding the cinched

waist tighter round, letting the *Blue Danube* float
through the perfect house, and feeling, in a pinch,
she'd have the sense to do what is right.

Yet, the maid wakes knotted in her covers, damp, uneasy
with the person in her body, unlike anyone
she'd imagined: Who am I? I

am who. It may have been the moon, but this night
a china body filled the doorway: her glazed cheeks,
rosy in the daylight, made

a rouged-up whore at night; the satin ribbons over
her shins had been unlaced, garters bit
at black stockings like cobwebs climbing

her sharp legs in mean arabesque. The maid,
thereafter vicious, tore open the curtains
to a light so hard, brilliant, nothing would look

clean. She scrubbed the morning like stained muslin
to erase the figurine and the truth
of being remade every day till she dies.

Still the rooms disappeared when she left them.

BLIGHT

The house cleaned, meals frozen, she was
ready to go. Like clockwork, when spring was
upon them, the mother took to her bed and dissolved.
Grief came on like an old film, a ticking reel
and a dusty spool of light; in washed-out yellows
and greens, the opening scene burrowed the dark
to a long shot of forsythia-pulp pulled out
of dormant limbs. These tugs of sorrow
she called vertigo, falling for days into years
of unpacking her deftly arranged cosmetics,
her matching luggage for college, the honeymoon, the hospitals.
Moving through her rooms in jagged silence, he'd let
the door slip, crash to the jamb. This perennial
spell was one more thing to drive poor Father
crazy. The daughter saw him grab her ankle once
and shake it hard. He called her *Queen*, said, *some people
have to work*. The mother couldn't hear his voice
from the foot of the bed where he hovered.
Bodies like theirs formed a mouth, she thought.
A peignoir of dogwood blooms drifted in the light.
Their wedding night they'd eaten crème brûlée in bed.
The blood in her temples thickened, flowered.
The Japanese maple trembled crimson spiders.
She didn't whine, she didn't close her eyes, she didn't rise.
Later, the daughter beside him folded
into the glove compartment, the trunk—under
the seats she slid; while through jaws
like a vise he cursed his family for seeing him
like this, then disappearing altogether. His hand

went right through her and battered the horn at each
house for the children to come OUT. When the last
door slammed, the mother counted her breaths above
the cool whirring air, replaying the childhood
scene where primrose and honeysuckle crawled
through her window that hepatitis summer. Listening
for the screen-click of her father from the garden,
his clothes prickly with okra and cucumber leaf,
she never got to twenty before he came
to her and in his hands, sweet with Lava soap,
a cool rag for her yellowing skin.

VANISHING POINT

—after Pierre Bonnard

Filling the house with blossoms (not blossoming)
he meant to draw her out, but she and her rooms
were inseparable. Beyond them something fierce had collected
against her, something gone untended like a hungry dog
or a dirty cut. From the sickening crowd's touch,
she traveled so far in, the interior became exterior
and the exterior vanished in the draperies.
All she asked of the world was to let her be
the audience, except of course, her painter who'd make her,
and make her forget the world. She'd move a certain way in the bath
and he'd say, please stop, please don't move, and she'd open
her self to the light for hours, crepe-blue eyes floating
to the sun he pulled indoors for her; everything, porcelain,
tile, and flesh, soaked with color onto his canvas.

At ten past five the perfumed rooms long for the weight
of his step. What if he never returns to paint her—
a lake that won't remember rain—to paint her—
slender, naked as the winter maple? She feels
a bump, a jostle, a rough hand to her wrist,
when through velvet and glass she sees her self
out there spinning round a sunny clearing of dandelion
and thrushes' down. *I've let this go too far,*
the painter's wife, pale with love for this
beautiful woman, caressed, made and remade
in the painter's hands—a tablet of ice loosened
from stone, in the frame of his arms held up
to the sun—she reaches for her again and again
as a mouth, a fountain's marble mouth,
reaches for the crystal leap of water.

ASTRONAUT

for Arturo Patten

The building is waiting for them; it exists for their sake, and, so long as it is there, they will be able to meet in the same manner. The space is theirs, even during the ebb, and in its emptiness it reminds them of the flood.
                                          —Elias Canetti

The world could explode and Rome
wouldn't know—it's built on air—

the fields could turn over
like an old mattress—I don't care

—made of salty water and craving
spaces to be beautiful as the rock's skin

breathes the river never ending—
it's not enough that hills fall in

to each other like fingers—we scale
the vacant building that waits for us

to begin—the heart is a moon
I'm breaking in

SLIDE

Snowballs tumble from the pines like fruit
from a dream of garbled voices two flights up.
The water glass is dry. You're buried in a drift,
seeing the bedroom with eyes closed and thinking
cool water down your throat before waking,
this isn't it, my life is bound to happen.
Sky slides off its blue ascent to break
and fall past your windows, eight on one wall,

looking for a way out. In the center
of the earth a tulip bulb shivers and tightens;
the ground lets go, its soil, boulders, grasses, trees
slipping down the hillside like a dress.
No one foresees the moment of release,
how much land will be taken in the slide
but it is bound to happen or unhappen.
You will surrender these rooms. Already

they swell imperceptibly with another's pulse,
another and another to come. Heat rises
from your skin, the snow-roof loosens, faults, slides
past the bedroom windows with the graceful
intent to change everything, a curtain
drawn back on the next scene in twenty years:
you're nearly sixty in the tropic of fingertips,
free of fevered expectations, mildly curious

where you might end up, but burning to know the weather
on Sunday. Will this be the week the ailanthus blooms?

MISSIONARY RIDGE

Wherever Sara went, flies followed
like cigarette smoke, flies followed her hands

talking to the cats at five a.m. in rooms
she lived in like a stained robe

for forty years with her big sister.
We'd cringe from below in our basement apartment

at the uninterrupted radio opera and wildlife shows,
the tubercular heaving before sunrise, their wet-wool smell.

In afternoons, still damp and salted from each other,
we'd hear about the bad winter coming,

sure to aggravate their bursitis and rheumatism.
At least they had each other and us to tend to.

Once through the kitchen window, I felt Sara's eyes
as I worked warm bread-dough: a shallow breath

on my shoulder, flies. How long had she been
there? Could she hear us this afternoon? Had she ever

hummed at another's touch, lost track of her own skin?
I liked that kind of sadness then.

We were couples linked at the edges,
negative to positive, absence to flood.

In October a famous surgeon bought our building
to turn it back into a home. The sisters found a place

they could afford under the overpass.
From a chair in the garage Sara watches the cars

but where's the drama in that, she smiles.
A year streams by as unaccounted for

as the rain down my kitchen window.
At six a.m. the garbage gets taken away,

and the girl next door comes out
to sit on her stoop with some coffee at around six thirty,

when my left foot hurts and this room's
buzz and hiss are bodiless.

NEST

Like a sunbather on the examining table,
she lets her eyes skim the windowblinds
—back and forth, east to west, slat by slat—
a machine gathering data. It helps
her breathe. She sees flickering in the cuts
of light, the roundness of a nest perhaps,
a sparrow's tail fans along the glass,
a dress barely touching the floor.
Though he's young, direct, sympathetic,
this doctor with enormous eyes,
she doesn't believe him and won't
have another test with a yes/no answer.
He says, something's wrong but,
he says, nothing's here but, she says,
there's the problem. She's not a body
hiding the truth. She's hiding herself
from the halogen, the culture, the slide,
the strangers passing her numbered cells
back and forth, east to west,
and the phone call, *negative*—every time
the stutter in her chest—but that's good,
good news, like bursting out of a packed train
after being felt up. Waiting for the papers
that say she can go, knowing she'll be back
in a month, she jerks up the blinds,
could make someone bleed, and there,
dozens of hornets, drugged in August heat,
circle and circle their papery catacombs,
the color of someone dying for years.

REACH

Having had all of nothing, every
bit of nothing, I've had enough.
My hand is over my mouth. Blue-throated
grackles pecking in the yard blink
in dismay. I sniff and circle youngish men
like ornamental deer but they're real
and move away to their secret lovelies
in alleyways abandoning green selves
to sunshine, to rain—red, purple, yellow,
boom boom boom. An early spring.
My heart is seriously green, sapling lean,
and grieving for crepe myrtles, their long skin
birthmarked, their higgledy-piggledy limbs
tied with bits of string—remember me.
Over the whole world lace is falling.
The Bradford pears are just beginning
their solemn procession two by two,
they blanch with happiness, and they reach
for each other across Carolina Avenue.
Take my hand from my mouth and I might start singing.

THE BED IS A STILL LIFE OF FLYING

She's driving her bed through an illustrated town
and the road snaps off like a pencil in her hands:
they hover, the bed and the girl in the covers,
and rise into a still life of sweeping through towers

and steeples, their shimmering wake like spun sugar.
Even the old daisies turn up.
Fumbling for something to steer by, slow,
or stop with, she's already falling, shredding

the air, the pull on her grave and enormous,
a snug emptiness down there feels like
a still life made for her. The bed
is a still life of pitching seas or dun water

just before the wake, still life of ardor unwaning,
still life of waning, still life of driving off bridges
in middle Tennessee, of every long shot at every
dartboard behind greasy doorknobs.

The bed is a still life of misunderstanding,
her head pulled back so her face slides off
into the dark between mattress and wall.
Still life of morning and scattershot sounds

of hundreds on the boardwalk: she's the child
shouting stop, stop, covering her ears to the careless
pounding up and down the pier, to boards straining
the tired frame. Still life, the body,

dense as an anvil tipped out of clouds.
Still life, light as a feather, a feather, she thinks,
going under again. Crickets work their music
through rain. The bed is a still life

of rain, six days and nights unceasing,
still life of floods creeping through soy fields,
water through velvet, violent water,
the sea means no harm and neither does he,

this next, other, last one, but she's
a split hull in the soy field.
Shallow breathing is still life,
being opened like wooden fruit,

being stars inside. The way blue
comes out of his eyes, she'd say
he was a still life of sky,
the way sleeping is a still life of dying,

the bed is a still life of flying,
while life waits still,
though mightily disheveled,
for her body to return.

CIPHERS

She's a walk at midnight when the train's long gone.
She's a smokestack lunging at three a.m. moonlight.
Streetcats wail and she unfurls like steam in your mouth.
Listening carefully to find what you've come for,
all the time what you thought she'd be and more,
she leaves abruptly and oh, how you cherish the ache,
how you crave the air for beauty uncomplicated, a singular
and a general want. Run your hand along the vessel
of her. Go ahead, she'll like it. You'll find her
empty in the right places, where she's full, no doubt
it's your doing. She wants to love you. Don't worry
that she closes her eyes when you're talking.
She's trying to remember what you look like
and keeps forgetting your name.

SIGHTING

A low-decibel ache,
buzzing in the joints,
love's only true
in the conditional present perfect,
says my mind, the sentence
tinkerer, gleeful dissector
of the heart who wouldn't touch
any of this. Shadow-mouse
in the corner of my eye,
ghost-darter by the roadside,
water like mercury in a lotus cup:
could you have loved me any less?

Just outside the porch light
a lawn chair hovers then tips,
sunflowers twirl ten feet
above the garden, there's hope
for the willow yet,
and a cloud like a continent
throwing its own light
against the purpling sky,
against my chest and it cracks:
the chairs in your parlor
seem empty and bare.

Six quarters tumbled down a metal chute,
a siren tightened and wailed, I reached in
to the bin for a paper and smelled bacon,
an ambulance was thrown like a discus,

the medic frowned, a map in his hands:
is your heart filled with pain?
I'm still reaching in, the world's
flash-frozen, my legs and arms
have darkened with bees, a hound
throws back his head and screams:
the blood-thrill of any beginning.
Shall I come back again?

Greased-leather crows startle
at the light, the chair, my body,
the garden's yellow spinning,
and into the pines they lift themselves:
one holds the answer
like a ruby in its mouth
it won't sing about, another
holds a virus from the Nile
that keeps slipping out (*tell me dear*),
has everything changed,
we still look the same,
are you lonesome tonight?

FOSSIL LOVE

My love has had to flee from me,
pray for amnesia and move to the city

he always hated, where summer smells
of rubber and gasoline, and winter's dirty

ice falls like tacks from doomsday buildings
where the sky stops.

My love has had to flee from me,
rub out my voice, my hands on his body.

Whole days and a field of memory
settle like sediment on our little fish:

last of the species she wanes nostalgic,
abandoning us, gill and fin,

to bedrock—a fossil smudged in dust,
her boneprint like a fist.

MINOR SEASON

From the creekbed widow
she gathers patience
misshapen stones to keep hands busy
a moon   a face   a mouth
scratched then cut
one stone into the other
taking hours or years of steady motion
the clock's faithfulness   unspoken
love in the backwoods
out of dead leaves and roots   dusk
crawls for the sky   ink on orange linen
days of pistachios, clementines, blue-bottled gin
come back   her life's calling
called again and again
the refrigerator gnaws through the morning
to noon hunched and scribbling at the desk
she's beginning to feel something   light
but not weightless
semi-transparent   one of no one
a mouth   a face   a moon   a circle encircled
fixed in blackberry winter

TO BE FIRE

One palm-sized stone on the deck
Rain-wet like we found it among the shore's incinerated flowers

That summer we'd strung a pail of stones out like candles on the railing
By morning they'd forgotten the sea

But I carried them with me place to place
In a bowl of water they'd flicker, seem to float with the old translucence

I have been in love some
After three days of rain this last stone is beautiful again

A bird skull of onyx
Get away sadness

I wrote water to be water
Over shiny stones worn down by the sun and my water-hands

I wanted to wear those stones like jewels around my waist
I wanted the stones to wear me like a blouse

I write field to be a field
A green drift over bones remembering

INTERLEAVING

Is wind the sound of crackling,
the burn of sudden winter. Is rain the sound
of slapping, the dissolute taste of silver.
Is field that steady reach of your longing
to fly, the dirt beneath surging in waves.
Am I your despair, and love a compound of symptoms.

Does wind bend and snap
young pines like pole beans, or is it pitched
through woodlands by planets, their cacophonies.
Is field that steady reach of your longing to fly.
Does rain collect itself and burst the seams of heaven—
you say I entered leaving—or was it thirst,

green and helpless, flooding us with good intentions.
Am I your despair, and love an insoluble crystal.
As field might exist to hold back the ocean,
I dread your steady reach. Like the shore,
I've a taste for disappearing.
My longing, this rage of dirt surging

in waves of I and thou, this measuring
of how wind is wind, rain rain,
we are finished and these are the elements:
cause and consequence, want and acquiescence—
they keep our periodic places. Need chooses me.
If I could go, I would never leave.

ATTRACTION

River lightning courses through denim-dark skies,
and a sheet floats above their bodies. A reach through cotton air,
his hand rests on her and there all of her goes
jittering, flocking, the self like steel filings
falls down the deep breath of electrons—his hand
moving now across her stomach—broken ice, a flash
of water knocking headlong through the brilliantine
desert—past pleasure and into the river, she's
a muslin rag, a map, a far stretch, first floating
and tugged by the current, then under the surface slipping,
nothing of her but what's held in his fingers—long muslin
pulled out and—dripping back into the water—held
there, translucent against the moon, folded over
again and again, twisted like rope, tightening, her skin
wrung out in his fists and unwound, a skein of warm silk,
a flush of wild geese, sudden blood. He's the ocean
dragging light, its afterself, across the sand;
she's the sand pulling him closer to houses like herons—
when their wings, their lips, taste the bitter
salts of chemistry, houses fly away.

PALM READER SEES LONG LOVE

You will reach the end of what
he will give. You'll circle the barbed wire
(a blind woman inside it),
around it you'll drive the borders
obsessively, cut into the quick,
hold your breath, wait in the dark
room, try to be the cleanest
pane of glass against it.
You'll walk nights across no-numbered
highways crisscrossing themselves,
sine and cosine, you'll squint and dash
for strips of green midriff between
asphalt—get to the other side.
You'll wander through towns between counties
where people whisper *see the crows
hammering inside her chest.* You reach
the end of what he will give and hold
the markers in your arms like kindling.
Opening the book of gibberish to begin
again through wet fields of sawgrass
you set out for the end of what
he will take, hoping it takes forever.

CAMEL STAMP

This camel represents uneasy transport
from desert to ocean, one life to another.
This camel represents memory, held in
so long even the camel forgets.

This camel has a very long neck to feel
the shiver of words for a very long time
and large eyes that see so much that isn't
there she wonders if she's even there.

This camel is a wonder and does everything
she's designed to do but she'd like to be long
instead of tall, slick instead of soft.
She'd like to be delivered, as in spoken,

set free. Tired of tasting air, this camel
thinks you would taste like water.

Notes

"Beast"—I feel sure the image of the tricycle in this poem came from C. K. Williams's poem, "The World's Greatest Tricycle-Rider," from his first book *Lies*; "When Memory Is Like That House in…"—I stole a line from Mark Strand, "I am a place, a place where things come together, then fly apart," which is from his poem "From a Lost Diary" in *The Continuous Life*; "Fish"—I quote St. Julian of Norwich by way of Eliot's "Little Gidding" and acknowledge Eliot in the poem; "Vanishing Point"—He might not remember it, but the last image in this poem was a gift from Fred Chappell; "The Bed Is a Still Life of Flying"—I took C. K. Williams's poem, "The Bed" (which uses a similar repeating form) from *The Vigil*, as a challenge and wrote my own; "Fossil Love"—The genesis of this poem comes from Sir Thomas Wyatt's "They flee from me, that sometime did me seek."

To be complete in my thanks to all who made it possible for me to write these poems over the past ten years would be to double the size of the book itself. Please accept this annotated version. My deepest thanks go to the Couch, Warren, Brewer, James, Wilson, and Fuselier families. I am grateful for the reassurance of my friends over a lifetime who are shining examples of what a good life looks like: Kathy and Jack Forde, Nicola and Christoph Niedermair, Katie Courtland, Theresa Pfarr, Clare Christie, Cheri and Jim Peters, Charles E. Richard, Karl Vandevender, Peter Guzzardi, and George and Susan Core. I have been lucky in friendships with writers whose work has not only brought me great happiness, but has spurred me on to do better: Cecily Parks, Leah Stewart, Matt O'Keefe, April Naoko Heck, Ann Patchett, William Henry Lewis, Chase Twichell, Russell Banks, Erin McGraw, Daniel Anderson, Juliana Gray, Greg Williamson, and Phil Stephens. And I have been unreasonably lucky in the teachers who have taken me to task again and again: thank you, Andrew Hudgins, Wyatt Prunty, Stuart Dischell, Fred Chappell, and Alan Shapiro. Finally, I am grateful to the fine people at the Virginia Center for the Creative Arts and the Kimmel Harding Nelson Center for the Arts for invaluable residencies.

About the Author

Leigh Anne Couch lives in Tennessee with her husband, Kevin Wilson, and is the managing editor of the *Sewanee Review*. Her poems have appeared in the *Western Humanities Review*, *Shenandoah*, *32 Poems*, *Blackbird*, *Carolina Quarterly*, *Alaska Quarterly Review*, and other journals. Her chapbook *Green and Helpless* was published in 2007 by Finishing Line Press. She has held residency fellowships at the Virginia Center for the Creative Arts and the Kimmel Harding Nelson Center for the Arts.